Teaching Tunes
Audiotape and Mini-Books Set
BASIC CONCEPTS

by Dr. Jean Feldman

SCHOLASTIC
PROFESSIONAL BOOKS

New York ♪ Toronto ♪ London ♪ Auckland ♪ Sydney ♪ Mexico City ♪ New Delhi ♪ Hong Kong

Dedication

These books are dedicated to all the children who don't
have a song in their heart—I give you one of mine!

Acknowledgments

Mark Dye has given my songs music and wings! I thank him for his musical genius, creativity, and commitment to FUN!

Alex Roswell, Sara Roswell, Stephanie Foss, and Jennifer Hiltz have added "childlike magic" to these songs. Thank you for your voices and your smiles.

I thank Liza Charlesworth for seeing the value in these books and for her dedication to giving children a reason to sing and read!

Danielle Blood has nurtured this project and brought it to life! I thank her for her enthusiasm, insight, leadership, and talents.

Maxie Chambliss's gifted hand has added the delightful and charming illustrations!

Thanks to the creative and thoughtful work of Ellen Matlach Hassell, who designed the book's interior, and Josué Castilleja who designed the cover.

And thanks to my mother, teachers, scout leaders, camp counselors, students, and colleagues who have shared these wonderful songs and ideas with me!

Music reminds us all that it is still a wonderful world and we have a lot to sing about!

Cover design by Josué Castilleja

Cover and interior illustrations by Maxie Chambliss

Interior design by Ellen Matlach Hassell
for Boultinghouse & Boultinghouse, Inc.

Product ISBN: 0-439-19937-9

Book ISBN: 0-439-19938-7

Contents

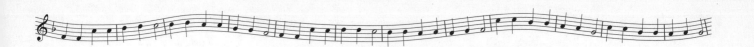

Introduction

Several years ago while I was visiting a kindergarten class, the teacher asked if I would like to hear her students read. Soon a small group of children had gathered around, eager to read me their simple mini-books, similar to the ones I have created for you here. I was amazed at the children's enthusiasm. Whether they had memorized the books isn't important—they thought they were reading, and that is what matters. I shared in their excitement and asked the teacher, "How did you teach your students to read so well?" The teacher had a twinkle in her eye as she answered, "Well, my children have discovered how much fun it is to read! And they're having so much fun, they want to read all the time!"

This story has two important lessons. First, we must show kids how much fun it is to read. Second, we must give children books that will allow them to experience reading success. This audiotape and mini-books set was created with these two goals in mind. Children love music, and they have always responded enthusiastically to my songs. Twelve of their favorite songs are included on the audiotape; the reproducible mini-books provide the song lyrics along with delightful illustrations that support the text. The combination of songs and mini-books makes reading fun for kids—and helps put them on the road to reading success.

Top 10 Reasons to Use This Book

♪ **Motivate children to read.** These songs and mini-books motivate children to read by showing them that reading is fun. Once they learn the songs, kids can "read along" in their own mini-books. Before long, they will be reading!

♪ **Build phonological awareness.** The rhythm, rhyme, and alliteration of these songs help children develop phonological awareness, an essential step in learning to read.

♪ **Help kids make the connection between the spoken word and print.** These songs reinforce the idea that "what I say can be written down, and what is written down I can read."

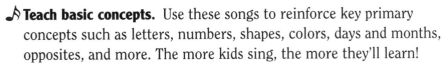

♪ **Help children learn to track and use picture clues.** The mini-books reinforce the concept of following a line of print from left to right. Children also learn to use picture clues to help them read the text.

♪ **Tap into diverse learning styles.** The combination of songs and mini-books works well for a variety of learning styles: There is singing for auditory learners, text and illustrations for visual learners, and suggested movements for kinesthetic learners.

♪ **Teach basic concepts.** Use these songs to reinforce key primary concepts such as letters, numbers, shapes, colors, days and months, opposites, and more. The more kids sing, the more they'll learn!

♪ **Provide take-home books.** Many children do not have access to books at home. These reproducible mini-books are a great way to help children build their own libraries. The books also provide a link between school and home, encouraging families to take part in the learning process and spend quality time together.

♪ **Enhance the classroom community.** Singing is a wonderful group activity that builds a sense of community. No matter what their reading level, all children will have fun joining in.

♪ **Develop small-motor skills.** Children build small-motor skills as they cut, color, and assemble the book pages in numerical order.

♪ **Have fun!** Children learn best when they're having fun. So start singing, smiling, reading, and learning!

People sing because they're happy, and they're happy because they sing! My hope is that these books will bring much happiness to your classroom. For additional information, please visit www.drjean.org.

Keep on singing!

Dr. Jean Feldman

How to Use This Book

Teaching Tunes Audiotape and Mini-Books Set: Basic Concepts can be integrated into any primary reading program and used in a number of ways. The songs and mini-books provide opportunities to teach a variety of reading skills, such as tracking a line of print, turning the page, using picture clues, identifying letters and high-frequency words, and sounding out words. They are designed for flexible use with individual children, partners, small groups, or the whole class.

Send-Home Mini-Books

Children love to share these songs and mini-books with their families. Send a letter to parents explaining the purpose of the mini-books and encouraging them to reinforce reading skills at home. (See the sample letter to families on page 9.) Children can create their own personal "libraries" in which to store their mini-books. Ask each child to bring to school an empty cereal box or other container. Let them decorate their container with wallpaper, wrapping paper, and other materials. As children make their mini-books, they can store them in their libraries.

Group Reading

Introduce the songs to children before they make their mini-books. (See How to Make the Mini-Books on page 8.) In this way, children will become familiar with the song lyrics and will be more motivated to read the books. To reinforce reading skills, write the song lyrics on sentence strips to place in a pocket chart. Try some of these suggestions for group reading experiences:

♪ **Choral Reading** Read together as you point to the words. (See page 7 for pointer ideas.)

♪ **Shadow Reading** You read a line, and then children repeat it.

♪ **Take a Turn** You read a line, children read the next line, and so on.

♪ **Magic Word** Select a particular word in the text. Every time you come to the magic word, children clap their hands, shout the word, or whisper the word.

Learning Centers

There are a number of ways that you can use the songs and mini-books in learning centers. Place the audiotape and mini-books in a listening center so children will have the opportunity to review the songs they enjoy most. Encourage partners to visit the listening center and sing the songs together. They can take turns singing alternate pages or they can sing the whole song together.

Sing-along mini-books are just one way to present song lyrics and build early literacy skills. Here are more ideas that are perfect for learning centers:

♪ **Big Books** Create oversized books to accompany the mini-books. You might use poster board cut in half, large paper grocery sacks, tagboard, or other materials. Use large handwriting or type for the lyrics. Have children illustrate the text.

♪ **Tag-Along Books** These are books that children can tote! Make a big book and punch two holes through the left side. Attach a pipe cleaner or a piece of yarn for a handle. (To display these, simply hang them with clothespins on a clothesline.)

♪ **Book Puzzles** Cut apart the book pages and trim off the page numbers. Glue the pages onto 5- by 6-inch sheets of construction paper. Invite children to arrange the pages in sequential order. (Store book puzzles in resealable plastic bags.)

♪ **Sing-Along Notebook** Make a song sheet for each mini-book. Have children illustrate the song sheets and then store the sheets in a three-ring binder. Use the songbook to entertain children during transitions, or let children take turns using the songbook as they lead a class sing-along. Invite other classes to visit, and let your students teach them the songs as well.

Using Pointers

Encourage children to use pointers to help them make the connection between the spoken word and printed word. Have children place a pointer on each word as they read or sing it. Before reading together as a group, give each student a pointer and do the following fun finger exercise. Have kids follow your movements with their own pointers as you say:

"Let's get the pointers
ready! Up!" Hold your pointer up.

"Down!" Hold your pointer down.

"All around!" Wiggle your pointer around.

"Attention!" Hold your pointer up straight.

"On the word!" Point to the first word in the book.

Here are a few kinds of pointers that children will enjoy using:

♪ **Wiggly Eye** Have each child glue a movable eye to the end of a craft stick. Challenge each child to "keep your eye on the word!"

♪ **Magic Pointer** Have each child dip the end of a craft stick in glue and then in glitter.

♪ **Plastic Fingernails** Give each child a plastic fingernail to glue to a craft stick. (Plastic fingernails often are sold around Halloween.)

♪ **Finger Puppet** Cut the fingers off several pairs of inexpensive cloth work gloves. Give each child one finger to decorate with fine-tip markers. Encourage kids to name their "finger buddies" and use them as pointers when they read.

♪ **Seasonal Pointers** Glue small seasonal erasers or stickers to craft sticks or straws.

Large pointers work well for reading together as a group. Copy the song lyrics onto sentence strips to use in a pocket chart. You might also make an oversized copy of the mini-books out of poster board or brown paper bags. Then use one of the following pointers as you read or sing together.

♪ **Stuffed Glove** Take a cloth work glove and color the tips with a red marker to look like fingernails. Stuff the glove with polyester fiberfill or cotton. Use a pipe cleaner to attach the glove to a paint stirrer or other stick. Use a glue gun to secure the glove in place. Then glue down four of the fingers, leaving the index finger pointing up.

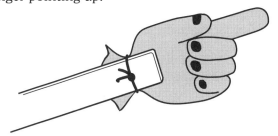

♪ **Magic Wand** Wrap aluminum foil around a cardboard tube from a pants hanger. Dip one end in glue and then in glitter.

How to Make the Mini-Books

These mini-books are designed for double-sided copying. If your machine does not have a double-sided function, make copies of the title page first. Then place these copies into the machine's paper tray. Next, make a copy of the second page so that page 2 copies directly behind the title page. (For 12- or 16-page books, copy the pages so that page 6 copies directly behind page 5.) For variety, copy some books on light-colored paper. Show children how to assemble their mini-books by following these steps:

1. Cut the page(s) in half along the solid line.

2. **For an 8-page book,** place pages 4/5 on top of pages 2/7, as shown.

   For a 12-page book, place pages 6/7 on top, followed by pages 4/9 and pages 2/11, as shown.

   For a 16-page book, place pages 8/9 on top, followed by pages 6/11, pages 4/13, and pages 2/15, as shown.

3. Fold the pages in half along the dotted line.

4. Check to be sure that the pages are in the correct numerical order. Then staple the pages together along the mini-book's spine.

5. Encourage children to personalize their books by coloring them with crayons, markers, or colored pencils.

Create your own mini-books using poems or other songs that children enjoy. Happy singing and reading!

8-page book

12-page book

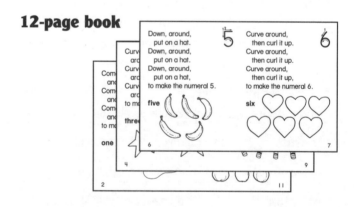

16-page book

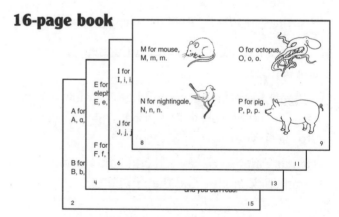

Date _____

Dear Family,

Our class is learning songs that teach important primary concepts such as numbers, letters, shapes, colors, opposites, and more. Each song comes with a mini-book that provides the song lyrics as well as illustrations that support the text. When children have learned the songs, they can read along in their mini-books. The rhyme and rhythm of the songs make them fun to sing—and help children as they are learning to read.

Your child will be excited to share these songs and mini-books with you. Most of the songs are set to simple, familiar tunes that are easy to learn. Please set aside time to enjoy these songs and books together. Here are some specific suggestions to make the most of this experience:

♪ Encourage your child to point to the words as he or she reads or sings them.

♪ Sing along with your child.

♪ Ask your child questions about the pictures. How do the pictures help your child know what the words are?

♪ Help your child decorate a shoe box or cereal box in which he or she can store the books.

♪ Take out the books from time to time and review them with your child.

♪ Encourage your child by commenting on how his or her reading is improving.

♪ Have fun! Follow your child's lead.

♪ Teach your child songs you remember from your own childhood.

Thank you for sharing this experience with your child.

Sincerely,

_____

Directions and Activities

The Shape Family

Purpose

Children learn the attributes and names of different shapes.

Directions

Using a large pointer, walk around the classroom and point to objects shaped like circles, triangles, squares, rectangles, ovals, and diamonds. Talk about the features of the different shapes (such as sides, angles, and curves). Let children take turns using the pointer as they identify various shapes around the room. Then sing "The Shape Family" for children, forming the shapes with your arms.

In advance, prepare a mini-book. Demonstrate how to follow along in the book as you sing. Have children make their own mini-books, following the directions on page 8. Ask children to look at the pictures and predict the words on each page. Sing the song again, modeling how to track words and encouraging children to do the same.

Activities...

♪ Play I Spy with shapes. For example, one child says, "I spy something that is shaped like a rectangle." The other children take turns guessing the object. The first child to guess correctly chooses the next object.

♪ Draw shapes with glue on heavy paper. Sprinkle the wet glue with dry flavored gelatin. When the glue has dried, children can scratch and sniff the shapes. (Note: Children should not share these. They will each need their own. This is a good opportunity to talk about germs.)

♪ Cut shapes from felt. Let children arrange the shapes on a flannel board to create various objects and designs.

♪ Invite children to draw shapes on the sidewalk with chalk.

♪ Have children "draw" shapes with their fingers on one another's backs and guess what they are.

♪ Divide the class into groups of four. Challenge each group to form different shapes with their bodies (standing or lying down). Take pictures of their shape formations and then compile the pictures to make a shape book.

♪ Invite children to form shapes with modeling clay.

♪ Cut geometric shapes from colored scrap paper. Have children glue these onto paper plates or sheets of construction paper to create a collage.

♪ Enjoy snacks of various shapes: square crackers, circular cookies, triangular nacho chips, and so on.

♪ Introduce children to three-dimensional shapes, such as cubes, cylinders, and spheres. Have children hold blocks, cans, balls, or other objects to reinforce these solid shapes.

Five Little Hot Dogs

Purpose

Children count backward and subtract by 1.

Directions

Ask your students, "Who likes hot dogs?" Sing "Five Little Hot Dogs." Clap your hands and bend

one finger each time you sing "Bam!" (For the last verse, close your fist to indicate that there are no hot dogs.) Have children assemble their mini-books. Then sing the song again, encouraging children to follow along in their books. Ask children to count the number of hot dogs on each page. Can they find the word that represents each number? Can they find the word "Bam!" on each page? Invite children to draw their favorite food in the pan on the last page.

Activities..

♪ Ask five volunteers to be hot dogs. Sing the song together. For each verse, point to a different hot dog to sing "Bam!" as he or she jumps up and then sits down.

♪ Without playing the tape, sing the song and vary the number of hot dogs in the pan.

♪ Make up similar songs about pancakes or popcorn. For example, "Five little pancakes frying in the pan. I flipped one over and away it ran." Or "Five popcorn kernels sizzling in the pot. The grease got hot and one went Pop!"

♪ Children will love a hot-dog snack called "Two Babies in a Bed." Slice a cooked hot dog lengthwise, open it, and place it on a piece of bread. Place a piece of cheese on top, as shown, and broil.

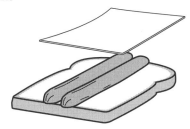

♪ Cut out felt hot dogs and buns. Place the felt shapes on a flannel board. Or attach magnetic tape to the back of the shapes and place them on a metal spatula.

The Numeral Song

Purpose

Children count objects and learn to write the numerals 1 to 10.

Directions

As you sing "The Numeral Song," trace the numerals in the air. (Remember to trace them backward if you are facing the class.) After singing the song a few times, have children assemble their mini-books. Have children use crayons to trace over the numeral on each page. Then sing the song again, encouraging children to follow along in their books.

Activities..

♪ Make textured numerals by writing them with glue on heavy paper. Then sprinkle the wet glue with glitter or dry flavored gelatin mix and let dry.

Teacher Tip

Make a simple flannel board from a piece of felt and a file folder. Staple closed the shorter sides of the file folder and then glue the felt onto the front. Store felt pieces inside the folder. A larger flannel board can be made from two 18- by 24-inch pieces of corrugated cardboard. Tape together the pieces at the top and then cover each side with felt or flannel. Poke holes through each side and tie together with 10-inch pieces of string, as shown, so that the board will stand on a tabletop.

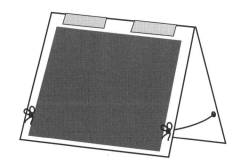

On heavy paper, write numerals with colored glue and let dry. (Colored glue can be purchased or made. Just add a few drops of food coloring to a bottle of white glue and shake.) Demonstrate how to make a rubbing: place a sheet of paper on top of the numeral and rub the side of a crayon across the numeral until the image is complete.

Copy, cut apart, and shuffle the mini-book pages. In your math center, tie a string between two chairs. Provide clothespins and invite children to hang the pages in numerical order on the string. Store the mini-book pages in a resealable plastic bag.

Let children practice writing numerals with a wet sponge on a chalkboard. They will also enjoy writing numerals with their fingers in shaving cream spread on a washable surface. (These ideas work well to reinforce letter formation as well.)

To make puzzle pieces, first cut paper plates in half. Write a numeral on one half of each plate. On the matching half, either draw the appropriate number of dots or write the number word, as shown. Make puzzle pieces for the numbers 1 to 10. Shuffle the pieces and invite children to match them.

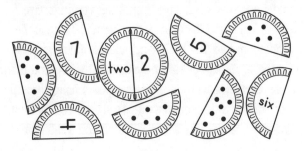

Give each child several pretzel sticks and twists. Challenge them to see how many numerals they can make from the twists and sticks. (All the numerals can all be made with a little nibbling!)

Hickory, Dickory, Dock

Purpose
Children read clocks. Children read text in quotation marks.

Directions
Sing "Hickory, Dickory, Dock" for children. As you sing about the mouse running up the clock, move your hands from your knees to your head. Clap your hands the number of chimes for each verse. After children make their mini-books, sing the song with children following along in their books. Call children's attention to the clock hands on each page. Ask them to identify the words that rhyme in each verse. Also have them locate the words in quotation marks.

Activities...

Help children make paper-plate clocks. In advance, lightly print the numerals 1 through 12 in pencil on the clock. Have children trace over the numerals with crayons or markers. Cut clock hands from colored construction paper and attach them to the middle of the plate with a brass fastener. As you sing each verse, invite children to move their clock hands to show the appropriate time.

Give children rhythm sticks or other instruments. Have them "chime" the hour in each verse with their instruments. Or have them chime the hour by tapping their fingers on a table, stomping their feet, blinking their eyes, and so on.

Display a digital clock next to a manual clock. Throughout the day, call children's attention to the two clocks and ask them to read the time.

As a group, brainstorm different ways to tell time. Ask children how they might tell the time if they didn't have a watch.

♪ Write the daily class schedule on chart paper, drawing clock faces to show activity times. Take pictures of children engaged in different activities and attach the pictures to illustrate the schedule.

♪ Give each child a long strip of paper. Have children make a time line of their day, from when they get up until when they go to bed.

My Letter Book

Purpose
Children review the alphabet and letter-sound associations.

Directions
Sing the traditional alphabet song with children. Explain that they will learn a new song to help them learn the letters and their sounds. Sing "My Letter Book" for children. Have children make their mini-books. Before stapling the books together, ask children to check the order of the pages. Display a written alphabet if they need help. Ask children to identify the animals on each page and then sing the song together.

Activities..

♪ Collect various alphabet books and invite children to compare them. Which is their favorite?

♪ Make a collaborative alphabet book. First, bind together 26 pages, each labeled with one letter of the alphabet. To make an *I Can Read Alphabet Book*, have children cut from magazines words that they can read. Then have them glue words starting with *A* to the *A* page, words starting with *B* to the *B* page, and so on. To make an *Alphabetical Friends Book*, attach photographs of children whose names begin with *A* to the *A* page, *B* to the *B* page, and so on.

You can make similar alphabet books with pictures of toys, sports, food, plants, holidays, and so on.

♪ Each day, choose a different letter to be the "magic password letter." Write the letter and hang it above the door to your classroom. Explain to children that they must whisper the letter sound every time they enter the classroom.

♪ Make a giant computer keyboard. Cut a shower-curtain liner in half. On one half of the liner, draw a keyboard with a permanent marker. (Use your computer keyboard as a reference.) As you call out letters, let children take turns swatting the letters with a flyswatter. They also can take turns swatting letters to spell their names and other words.

Color Word Farm

Purpose
Children spell color words and review farm animals.

Directions
Sing "Color Word Farm" for children, inviting them to join in when they feel ready. Then have children make their mini-book and color the animals the appropriate colors. Call their attention to the animal and color word on each page. Sing the song again, encouraging children to follow along in their books.

Activities..

♪ Make stick puppets to use as props while singing. Color and cut out the animals on each page. Then staple the animals to straws and give each child a puppet. Sing the song together and have kids hold up their puppet when you reach the verse about that animal.

As you sing, do "letter aerobics" to spell out the color words. If a letter is small (such as *e, s,* and *w*), clap in front of you. If a letter is tall (such as *t, l,* and *k*), clap high. If it has a "tail" (such as *y, p,* and *j*), clap low. For example, this is how you would spell *purple* with letter aerobics:

p	clap low
u	clap in front
r	clap in front
p	clap low
l	clap high
e	clap in front

To make color-word puzzles, write each color word on a sentence strip. Cut apart the letters of each word and store them in an envelope labeled with the color word. Children remove the letters and arrange them in the proper order. They can self-check by looking at the front of the envelope.

Make up additional verses about other animals, such as a gray donkey, a pink fish, a white mouse, or a tan goat.

Sing the letters in children's names to the tune of "Bingo."

Dismiss children to a new activity by spelling color words. When you spell the color of a child's clothing, he or she is dismissed to the next activity.

Print color words on the chalkboard or chart paper. Trace around the outside of each word, as shown. Have children study and compare the configuration of various color words.

Teddy Bear

Purpose

Children learn positional words.

Directions

As you sing "Teddy Bear" to children, use a teddy bear to act out the motions in the song. Then invite children to stand, sing, and act out the motions. Have children assemble their mini-books and call their attention to the illustrations on each page. Have them predict what the words will say. Ask them to identify the rhyming words. Sing the song again together, encouraging children to point to the words as they sing them.

Activities...

Give each child an enlarged photocopy of the mini-book cover. Have kids color, cut out, and tape the bear onto a craft stick. Call out directions and ask children to move their bears accordingly. For example, say, "Put your bear on your head. Put your bear beside you. Put your bear between your ankles. Put your bear under your chin."

Plan a teddy bear parade. Ask children to bring their favorite teddy bear or stuffed animal from home. (Be sure to have several extras on hand for children who don't bring animals from home.) Sing "Teddy Bear" and have children use their toys to act out the motions. Play music and invite children to march around the classroom with their toys. For a math lesson, have kids count the toys, sort them, graph them by type, and so on.

Make a big book version of the mini-book. Type the words in a large font and glue the text onto each page. Have children add illustrations. Punch holes on the left side and bind the pages together with ribbon or yarn.

The Opposite Song

Purpose
Children learn opposites and positional words.

Directions
Sing "The Opposite Song" for children, acting out the opposite words. Sing the song again, inviting children to join in when they feel ready. Then ask children if they can guess the meaning of the word *opposite*. Ask them to think of other opposites that are not included in the song. List their ideas on chart paper or on the chalkboard. Have children assemble their mini-books. Sing the song again with children following along in their books.

Activities...

♪ Add more verses to the song using the list of opposites from the above activity. Ask children to think of movements to go with the new verses and then sing them together.

♪ Make a *Book of Opposites* for your classroom library. Give each child a piece of paper that is folded in half. Ask each child to think of two opposite words. Have them write or dictate the words and then draw an illustration for each. Compile the pages, add a cover, and staple the pages together.

♪ Play the Opposite Game. Say a word, and then children say and act out the opposite. For example, if you say *tall*, children stoop down and say *short*. If you say *laugh*, children say *cry* as they pretend to cry.

♪ Explain that opposites are also called antonyms. Then explain that words that have the same meaning are called synonyms. On chart paper or on the chalkboard, write a common word such as *big*. Ask children to suggest synonyms and write these in a web around the word. Add additional words along with simple illustrations.

All You Lucky Children!

Purpose
Children learn the days of the week and food words. Children are introduced to sequence and pattern in the lyrics.

Directions
As you sing "All You Lucky Children!" make the following motions for each food:

Sunday	Put your hands in your armpits and flap like a chicken.
Monday	Extend your left hand and pretend to spread peanut butter on it with your right hand.
Tuesday	Snap your fingers.
Wednesday	Pretend to slurp a spoonful of soup.
Thursday	Pretend to lick an ice cream cone.
Friday	Clap your hands.
Saturday	Hold your palm over your head as if you were carrying a pizza.

Have children assemble their mini-books. Then play the song a second time as children follow along in their books. When they are familiar with the words, review the motions and sing the song together.

Activities...

♪ Make a visual aid for children to use as they sing this song. Write each day of the week and its corresponding food on a paper plate. Let children draw pictures of the foods on the plates. Ask seven volunteers to hold the plates and stand in order from Sunday to Saturday. Sing the song as a group. Have the volunteers hold up their plate when you reach the verse about their day.

♪ Ask children to find the days of the week on the classroom calendar.

♪ Think of an adjective that begins with the same letter as each day of the week—for example, Marvelous Monday, Terrific Tuesday, Wonderful Wednesday, Thrilling Thursday, Fabulous Friday, Super Saturday, and Sensational Sunday. Use these adjectives each morning as you review the daily schedule with students.

♪ Sing "Here We Go 'Round the Mulberry Bush," making up words for each day. For example, "This is the way we read our books, read our books, read our books. This is the way we read our books, so early Monday morning." For the other days of the week, you could paint a picture, build with blocks, share with friends, run and play, and so on. Add movements to go with the new verses.

Months of the Year

Purpose
Children learn the order of the months.

Directions
Remind children that you can learn anything with a song! Explain that you will teach them a simple song that will help them remember the order of the months. Sing the song for children and then have them assemble their mini-books. After they've made their books, review the words together. Ask them what the illustrations represent. Then ask them to find the month in which they were born. Have them find the months of each season. Sing the song again, encouraging children to point to the words as they sing.

Activities

♪ Teach children the motions of the macarena to go with the months:

January	Extend right hand, palm down.
February	Extend left hand, palm down.
March	Turn right hand, palm up.
April	Turn left hand, palm up.
May	Place right hand on left shoulder.
June	Place left hand on right shoulder.
July	Place right hand on back of head.
August	Place left hand on back of head.
September	Place right hand on left hip.
October	Place left hand on right hip.
November	Place right hand on right side of back.
December	Place left hand on left side of back.
New Year	Turn around.

♪ Make a class quilt with a square for each month of the year. Cut twelve 12-inch squares from heavy paper. Write a month on each square. Have children work in groups to decorate the month in which they were born. Punch holes in the corners and tie the squares together with yarn, as shown.

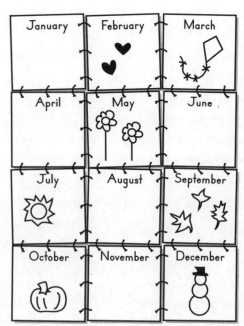

♪ Have children record the events of each school day in a collaborative class journal. Make a journal for each month. Each day, choose a child to draw a picture or write about events of that day.

♪ Make a time line to document special activities that take place throughout the school year. Write the months in large letters. Attach photographs or children's drawings to illustrate the text.

What's the Weather?

Purpose
Children learn to spell weather words.

Directions
Invite children to look out the window and describe the weather. Ask them how they can find out what the weather will be like tomorrow. Ask who watches the weather report on television and who listens to the radio. Explain that a meteorologist is a person who studies the weather.

Sing "What's the Weather?" for children. Sing the song again, inviting children to join in when they are ready. Then have children assemble their mini-books. Review the books together, asking children to identify words and spell them out. Invite them to draw the current weather on the last page. Sing the song while children read and sing along.

Activities

♪ Print weather words on sentence strips and place them in a pocket chart. Point to the letters as you spell out the words.

♪ Bring in the weather section from the newspaper. Discuss what the symbols mean for each type of weather.

♪ Invite your local television or radio meteorologist to visit your school.

♪ Choose one child each day to be the meteorologist and to lead the class in the song. As they sing, have children put their thumbs down if a verse does not describe that day's weather. Have them put their thumbs up if a verse does describe that day's weather.

♪ Let children brainstorm how to have fun on a rainy day!

♪ Place a large thermometer outside your classroom window. Encourage children to check the temperature several times a day. For a group math activity, graph the temperature throughout the day.

Special Me!

Purpose
Children build self-esteem as they think about what makes them special. Children personalize their books with illustrations.

Directions
Sing "Special Me!" for children. Discuss the different ways that people are special. Ask each child to think of one characteristic that makes him or her special. Then have children assemble their mini-books. Explain to children that they will make their mini-book special by drawing their own unique pictures. Read aloud the directions on each page. Sing the song again, challenging children to point to the words on each page. Have children share their books with their classmates and families.

Activities

♪ Make a collaborative class book titled *I Can Do Something Special*. Have each child draw a picture of something that he or she can do well. Ask children to write or dictate a sentence about their drawing.

♪ Use a T-chart to compare and contrast how people are alike and different.

♪ For a math lesson, graph the similarities and differences of class members. For example, graph children's eye color, the number of family members they each have, the number of teeth they have each lost, and so on.

♪ Ask each child to bring to school a baby picture. Attach a self-sticking note with the child's name to the back of the picture. Show the pictures one at a time to the class. Can they guess who each "beautiful baby" has grown up to be? How have they changed?

♪ Place a small mirror in a shoe box. Tell children that the most wonderful thing in the world is inside the box. It's so unique that there is only one like it in the whole world! Ask them to pass around the box and peek inside. Ask them not to talk so that each child is surprised by what's inside.

♪ Choose one child each week to be the "superstar." Make a poster or attribute web about that child. Let the superstar choose a story or song, or lead the class during circle time.

We are the shapes
that you all know.
Look for us wherever you go!

The Shape Family

Tune: "I'm a Little Teapot"

I am brother oval,
shaped like a zero.

I am baby triangle.
Three sides have I.

I am momma circle,
round like a pie.

I'm sister diamond,
with a sparkle and a glow.

I am papa square.
My sides are four.

I'm cousin rectangle,
shaped like a door.

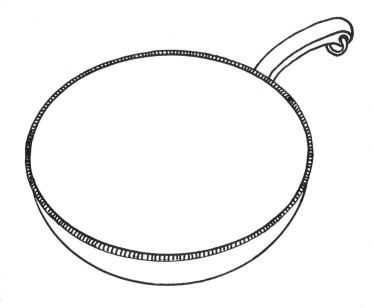

In the pan, draw a food you like to eat.

8

Five Little Hot Dogs

Tune: "Three Little Fishies"

I

One little hot dog
   frying in the pan.
The grease got hot,
   and one went BAM!

(Repeat.)

6

Four little hot dogs
   frying in the pan.
The grease got hot,
   and one went BAM!

(Repeat.)

3

Five little hot dogs
  frying in the pan.
The grease got hot,
  and one went BAM!

(Repeat.)

No little hot dogs
  frying in the pan.
The grease got hot,
  and the pan went BAM!

(Repeat.)

Three little hot dogs
  frying in the pan.
The grease got hot,
  and one went BAM!

(Repeat.)

Two little hot dogs
  frying in the pan.
The grease got hot,
  and one went BAM!

(Repeat.)

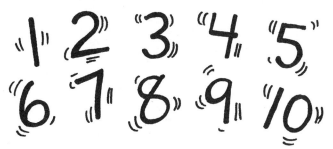

We can sing the
   numeral song.
We can sing the
   numeral song.
We can sing the
   numeral song
and make numerals
   all day long!

12

Teaching Tunes Audiotape and Mini-Books Set: Basic Concepts   Scholastic Professional Books

The Numeral Song

Tune:
"Skip to My Lou"

1

Make a circle,
   then a line.
Make a circle,
   then a line.
Make a circle,
   then a line,
to make the numeral 9.

nine

10

Curve around and
   slide to the right.
Curve around and
   slide to the right.
Curve around and
   slide to the right,
to make the numeral 2.

two

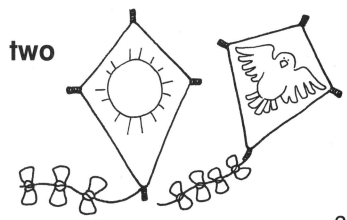

3

Come right down
    and that is all.
Come right down
    and that is all.
Come right down
    and that is all,
to make the numeral 1.

one

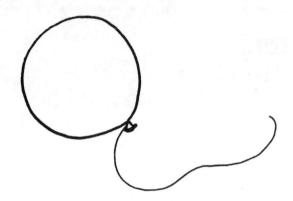

2

Come right down,
    then make a zero.
Come right down,
    then make a zero.
Come right down,
    then make a zero,
to make the numeral 10.

ten

11

Curve in and
    around again.
Curve in and
    around again.
Curve in and
    around again,
to make the numeral 3.

three

4

Make an S, then
    close the gate.
Make an S, then
    close the gate.
Make an S, then
    close the gate,
to make the numeral 8.

eight

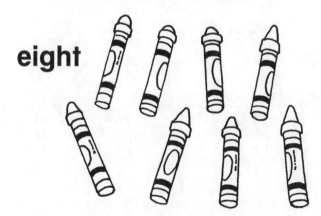

9

Slide to the right
   and slant it down.
Slide to the right
   and slant it down.
Slide to the right
   and slant it down,
to make the numeral 7.

seven

8

Teaching Tunes Audiotape and Mini-Books Set: Basic Concepts   Scholastic Professional Books

Down, over,
   down some more.
Down, over,
   down some more.
Down, over,
   down some more,
to make the numeral 4.

four

5

Down, around,
  put on a hat.
Down, around,
  put on a hat.
Down, around,
  put on a hat,
to make the numeral 5.

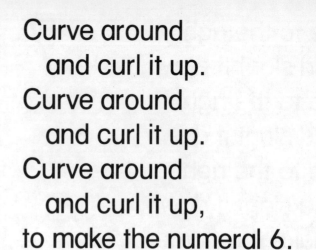

five

6

Curve around
  and curl it up.
Curve around
  and curl it up.
Curve around
  and curl it up,
to make the numeral 6.

six

7

Hickory, dickory, dock.
The mouse ran up the clock.
The clock struck twelve.
"I'm proud of myself!"
Hickory, dickory, dock.
Tick tock!

12

Hickory, Dickory, Dock

Teaching Tunes Audiotape and Mini-Books Set: Basic Concepts   Scholastic Professional Books

Hickory, dickory, dock.
The mouse ran up the clock.
The clock struck one.
The mouse said, "What fun!"
Hickory, dickory, dock.

1

Hickory, dickory, dock.
The mouse ran up the clock.
The clock struck ten.
"We're near the end!"
Hickory, dickory, dock.

10

Hickory, dickory, dock.
The mouse ran up the clock.
The clock struck three.
The mouse said, "Whoopee!"
Hickory, dickory, dock.

3

Hickory, dickory, dock.
The mouse ran up the clock.
The clock struck two.
The mouse said, "Yahoo!"
Hickory, dickory, dock.

Hickory, dickory, dock.
The mouse ran up the clock.
The clock struck eleven.
The mouse said,
   "We're sizzling!"
Hickory, dickory, dock.

Hickory, dickory, dock.
The mouse ran up the clock.
The clock struck four.
The mouse said, "Do more!"
Hickory, dickory, dock.

Hickory, dickory, dock.
The mouse ran up the clock.
The clock struck nine.
The mouse said, "So fine!"
Hickory, dickory, dock.

Hickory, dickory, dock.
The mouse ran up the clock.
The clock struck eight.
The mouse said, "It's great!"
Hickory, dickory, dock.

8

Hickory, dickory, dock.
The mouse ran up the clock.
The clock struck five.
The mouse said, "Let's jive!"
Hickory, dickory, dock.

5

Teaching Tunes Audiotape and Mini-Books Set: Basic Concepts   Scholastic Professional Books

Hickory, dickory, dock.
The mouse ran up the clock.
The clock struck six.
The mouse said,
  "Fiddlesticks!"
Hickory, dickory, dock.

6

Hickory, dickory, dock.
The mouse ran up the clock.
The clock struck seven.
The mouse said,
  "Oh, heavens!"
Hickory, dickory, dock.

7

Write your name and other words that you can read.

16

My Letter Book

Tune: "Short'nin' Bread"

Teaching Tunes Audiotape and Mini-Books Set: Basic Concepts   Scholastic Professional Books

Aa

Zz

1

Y for yak,
Y, y, y.

Z for zebra,
Z, z, z.

14

C for cat,
C, c, c.

D for dog,
D, d, d.

3

A for alligator,
A, a, a.

B for bear,
B, b, b.

Letter sounds are
all you need.
Put them together
and you can read!

E for
elephant,
E, e, e.

W for walrus,
W, w, w.

F for fish,
F, f, f.

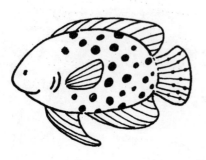

X for x-ray,
X, x, x.

U for umbrella bird,
U, u, u.

V for vulture,
V, v, v.

G for goat,
G, g, g.

H for horse,
H, h, h.

Teaching Tunes Audiotape and Mini-Books Set: Basic Concepts   Scholastic Professional Books

Q for quail,
Q, q, q.

R for rabbit,
R, r, r.

K for
kangaroo,
K, k, k.

L for lion,
L, l, l.

I for iguana,
I, i, i.

S for seal,
S, s, s.

J for jaguar,
J, j, j.

T for turtle,
T, t, t.

M for mouse,
M, m, m.

O for octopus,
O, o, o.

N for nightingale,
N, n, n.

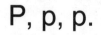

P for pig,
P, p, p.

There was a farmer
had a cat and
Black was her name-o.
   B-L-A-C-K
   B-L-A-C-K
   B-L-A-C-K
And Black was her name-o.

8

Color Word Farm

Tune: "Bingo"

There was a farmer
had a dog and
Brown was his name-o.
   B-R-O-W-N
   B-R-O-W-N
   B-R-O-W-N
And Brown was his name-o.

1

Teaching Tunes Audiotape and Mini-Books Set: Basic Concepts   Scholastic Professional Books

There was a farmer
had a chick and
Yellow was her name-o.
   Y-E-L-L-O-W
   Y-E-L-L-O-W
   Y-E-L-L-O-W
And Yellow was her name-o.

6

There was a farmer
had a frog and
Green was his name-o.
   G-R-E-E-N
   G-R-E-E-N
   G-R-E-E-N
And Green was his name-o.

3

There was a farmer
had a cow and
Purple was her name-o.
    P-U-R-P-L-E
    P-U-R-P-L-E
    P-U-R-P-L-E
And Purple was her name-o.

There was a farmer
had a pig and
Red was his name-o.
    R-E-D
    R-E-D
    R-E-D
And Red was his name-o.

There was a farmer
had a duck and
Orange was her name-o.
    O-R-A-N-G-E
    O-R-A-N-G-E
    O-R-A-N-G-E
And Orange was her name-o.

There was a farmer
had a bird and
Blue was his name-o.
    B-L-U-E
    B-L-U-E
    B-L-U-E
And Blue was his name-o.

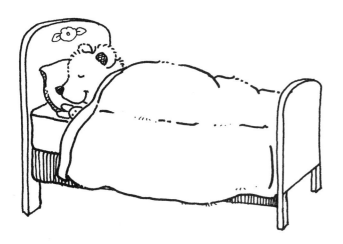

Teddy Bear,
Teddy Bear,
say, "Good night!"

Teaching Tunes Audiotape and Mini-Books Set: Basic Concepts   Scholastic Professional Books

Teddy Bear

Tune: "Turkey in the Straw"

Teddy Bear,
Teddy Bear,
turn around.

Teddy Bear,
Teddy Bear,
say your prayers.

Teddy Bear,
Teddy Bear,
read the news.

Teddy Bear,
Teddy Bear,
touch the ground.

2

Teddy Bear,
Teddy Bear,
turn off the light.

7

Teddy Bear,
Teddy Bear,
tie your shoes.

4

Teddy Bear,
Teddy Bear,
go upstairs.

5

Hot and cold,
hot and cold,
hot and cold,
and give a little clap.

hot cold

Teaching Tunes Audiotape and Mini-Books Set: Basic Concepts Scholastic Professional Books

8

The Opposite Song

Tune: "Short'nin' Bread"

We can do opposites,
opposites, opposites.
We can do opposites.
Follow me!

I

Up and down,
up and down,
up and down,
and give a little clap.

up

down

6

Front and back,
front and back,
front and back,
and give a little clap.

front back

3

Top and bottom,
top and bottom,
top and bottom,
give a little clap.

top

bottom

Open and shut,
open and shut,
open and shut,
and give a little clap.

open   shut

Happy and sad,
happy and sad,
happy and sad,
and give a little clap.

happy   sad

Left and right,
left and right,
left and right,
and give a little clap.

left   right

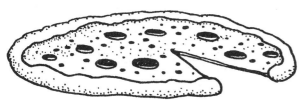

Today is Saturday.
Saturday pizza,
Friday hot dogs,
Thursday ice cream,
Wednesday soup,
Tuesday snap beans,
Monday peanut butter,
Sunday chicken,
all you lucky children!
Well, that's okay!

8

All You Lucky Children!

Tune: "Today Is Monday"

1

Today is Thursday.
Thursday ice cream,
Wednesday soup,
Tuesday snap beans,
Monday peanut butter,
Sunday chicken,
all you lucky children!
Well, that's okay!

6

Today is Monday.
Monday peanut butter,
Sunday chicken,
all you lucky children!
Well, that's okay!

3

Teaching Tunes Audiotape and Mini-Books Set: Basic Concepts   Scholastic Professional Books

Today is Sunday.
Sunday chicken,
all you lucky children!
Well, that's okay!

2

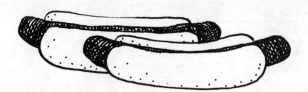

Today is Friday.
Friday hot dogs,
Thursday ice cream,
Wednesday soup,
Tuesday snap beans,
Monday peanut butter,
Sunday chicken,
all you lucky children!
Well, that's okay!

7

Today is Tuesday.
Tuesday snap beans,
Monday peanut butter,
Sunday chicken,
all you lucky children!
Well, that's okay!

4

Today is Wednesday.
Wednesday soup,
Tuesday snap beans,
Monday peanut butter,
Sunday chicken,
all you lucky children!
Well, that's okay!

5

Happy New Year!

8

Months of the Year

Tune: "Ten Little Indians"

Teaching Tunes Audiotape and Mini-Books Set: Basic Concepts   Scholastic Professional Books

I

September,

October,

6

March,

April,

3

January,

February,

November,

December,

May,

June,

July,

August,

Draw the weather outside your window today.

8

What's the Weather?

Tune: "Clementine"

1

Windy, windy,
windy, windy,
it is windy in the sky.
W-I-N-D-Y, windy,
it is windy in the sky.

6

Cloudy, cloudy,
cloudy, cloudy,
it is cloudy in the sky.
C-L-O-U-D-Y, cloudy,
it is cloudy in the sky.

3

Sunny, sunny,
sunny, sunny,
it is sunny in the sky.
S-U-N-N-Y, sunny,
it is sunny in the sky.

Snowy, snowy,
snowy, snowy,
it is snowy in the sky.
S-N-O-W-Y, snowy,
it is snowy in the sky.

Rainy, rainy,
rainy, rainy,
it is rainy in the sky.
R-A-I-N-Y, rainy,
it is rainy in the sky.

Foggy, foggy,
foggy, foggy,
it is foggy in the sky.
F-O-G-G-Y, foggy,
it is foggy in the sky.

Very Important Person

Name_____

Eye Color

_____

Hair Color

_____

Age

_____

Fill in the information.
In the box, draw a picture
of yourself.

8

Teaching Tunes Audiotape and Mini-Books Set: Basic Concepts   Scholastic Professional Books

Special Me!

Tune:
"Twinkle, Twinkle, Little Star"

I

Special, special, special me,

Draw a picture of you with a
friend.

6

I'm as special as can be!

Draw something you do well.

3

Special, special, special me,

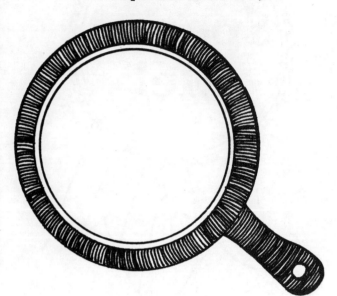

In the mirror, draw a picture of yourself.

2

I'm as special as can be!

In the star, draw one of your favorite things.

7

There is no one quite like me.

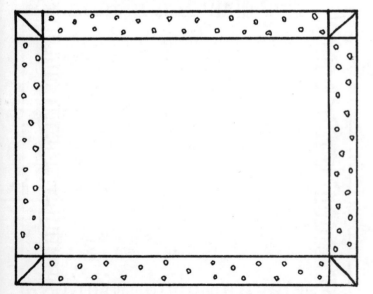

Draw a picture of you with a family member.

4

I'm as good as I can be!

Draw a picture of something you like to do at school.

5